LEVEL 2

Deadly Predators

Melissa Stewart

NATIONAL GEOGRAPHIC

Washington, D.C.

For Tali, one of my favorite predators —M. S.

The publisher and author gratefully acknowledge the expert review of this book
by Dr. Bill Swanson of the Cincinnati Zoo in Cincinnati, Ohio, U.S.A.

SECRET LIFE OF
PREDATORS

As seen on the National Geographic Channel

Design by YAY! Design

ISBN: 978-1-4263-1346-2 (Paperback)
ISBN: 978-1-4263-1347-9 (Library)

Photo credits

Cover, Brand X/Getty Images; 1, Sandy Flint/National Geographic My Shot; 2, Kevin Horan/Getty Images; 4, Alaska Stock/Corbis; 7 (UP), Hans Reinhard/Science Source; 7 (LOLE), Jim and Jamie Dutcher/National Geographic My Shot; 7 (LORT), Picture Press/Alamy; 8, Photo Researchers RM/Getty Images; 8-9, Martin Vavra/National Geographic My Shot; 10, Paul Jarvis/National Geographic My Shot; 11, Kathleen Reeder/National Geographic My Shot; 12–13, Richard Ress/National Geographic My Shot; 14, Photo Researchers RM/Getty Images; 15 (UP), Anthony Bannister/Gallo Images/Corbis; 15 (CTR), Mint Images RM/Getty Images; 15 (LO), Giovanni Antonio Diaz/National Geographic Stock; 16, Mike Parry/Minden Pictures; 18–19, Amos Nachoum/Corbis; 18 (INSET), Sue Flood/npl/Minden Pictures; 20 (UP), Computer Earth/Shutterstock; 20 (UP CTR), Rob Wilson/Shutterstock; 20 (LOCTR), Tom Brakefield/Corbis; 20 (LO), Flickr RF/Getty Images; 21 (UP), Vincent Grafhorst/Foto Natura/Minden Pictures; 21 (LE CTR), risteski goce/Shutterstock; 21 (RT CTR), Walter Nussbaumer/National Geographic My Shot; 21 (LO), Aimee Woodbury/National Geographic My Shot; 22, Bianca Lavies/National Geographic Stock; 24, Thierry Lombry/National Geographic My Shot; 26, Manny Ramirez/National Geographic My Shot; 27, Austin Thomas/National Geographic My Shot; 28–29, Anup Shah/naturepl.com; 30 (UP), Eduard Kyslynsky/Shutterstock; 30 (CTR), AnetaPics/Shutterstock; 30 (LO), Ellen C/Shutterstock; 31 (4 UP LE), Photo Researchers RM/Getty Images; 31 (4 UP RT), Visuals Unlimited/Getty Images; 31 (4 LO LE), Flickr RF/Getty Images; 31 (4 LO RT), rujithai/Shutterstock; 31 (5), Simon Pidcock/National Geographic My Shot; 31 (6 UP), Siddhardha Gargie/National Geographic My Shot; 31 (6 LE), Paul Jarvis/National Geographic My Shot; 31 (6 RT), Amos Nachoum/Corbis; 31 (6 LO), skynetphoto/Shutterstock; 31 (7), Mike Parry/Minden Pictures; 32 (UPLE), Bianca Lavies/National Geographic Stock; 32 (UPRT), Kavun Kseniia/Shutterstock; 32 (LE CTR), Olga Selyutina/Shutterstock; 32 (RT CTR), EastVillage Images/Shutterstock; 32 (LOLE), Aimee Woodbury/National Geographic My Shot ; 32 (LORT), Science Faction/Getty Images

Printed in the United States of America
14/WOR/2

Table of Contents

Hungry Hunters

Grizzly bears eat fish and other small animals. They usually weigh 300 to 500 pounds. The largest bears can weigh 800 pounds!

Wolves chase.
Sharks attack.
Bears lunge.

All these animals are predators. They're all after the same thing.

Meat. They need it to live and grow.

Word Bite

PREDATOR: An animal that hunts and eats other animals

Dogs in the Wild

Wolves are members of the dog family. So are foxes, coyotes, and African wild dogs. All of these dogs are powerful predators.

Big ears help wild dogs hear their prey. Sensitive noses help the dogs sniff out food.

Wild dogs also have large teeth and strong jaws. They can kill prey larger than themselves.

Word Bite
PREY: An animal that is eaten by another animal

A coyote has 42 teeth. Some can tear flesh. Others can crush bone.

African wild dogs hunt in packs.

An arctic fox stalks its prey.

Cats in the Wild

Thirty-six kinds of cats live in the wild. And they're all expert hunters.

The rusty-spotted cat is the smallest. It weighs less than a half-gallon jug of milk.

The rusty-spotted cat lives in India. At night, it hunts for birds, mice, lizards, and frogs.

Q What happened when the tiger swallowed a ball of yarn?

A It had mittens.

What is the biggest cat in the world? The Siberian tiger. It can weigh more than three large men.

Siberian tigers can eat up to 80 pounds of meat at one time.

Female lions hunt in a group. They work together to get a meal.

Most cats live alone. But lions live in a family group called a pride.

The males protect the group. The females do all the hunting.

Word Bite
PRIDE: A family group of lions

A cougar has long, strong legs. But it can't run fast or far. It sneaks up on prey. Then it jumps on the animal and bites its neck.

Cougars have sharp teeth. They chop prey into bite-size bits.

Polar Power

The polar bear is the largest bear in the world. It's also the most deadly. Polar bears use their sharp teeth and huge paws to catch prey.

A polar bear has one of the world's best noses. It comes in handy when sniffing out dinner.

Q What do you call a polar bear with earmuffs?

A Whatever you want. It can't hear you!

They hunt alone. Polar bears mostly eat seals snatched from holes in the ice. But sometimes they eat small animals, too.

Mini-monsters

These predators may be small, but they sure are deadly!

Giant Water Bug
A giant water bug hunts fish and frogs, snakes and snails. It jabs prey with its mouthparts. Then it sucks out the animal's insides!

Wind Scorpion

This little critter has huge jaws and runs like the wind. It chases down termites, beetles, and even lizards. This one caught a cricket.

Short-tailed Shrew

This shrew's spit is full of venom. The shrew uses the spit to paralyze its prey.

Army Ants

A group of army ants looks like a moving carpet. The group can be as wide as a street. It can be as long as a football field. The ants kill and eat everything in their path.

Word Bite

PARALYZE: To make unable to move

VENOM: A liquid some animals make that is used to kill or paralyze other animals

Ocean Hunters

The great white shark can go weeks without eating. But when it gets hungry . . . look out!

The fierce fish has up to 3,000 teeth. It uses them to grab fish, seals, sea lions, and dolphins.

A great white shark attacks from below. It may push up with so much power that it rises out of the water.

Orcas attack a gray whale.

Orcas have two ways of hunting. They can surround a large animal and attack as a group. Then they share the meal.

Q Why did the orca cross the ocean?

A To get to the other tide.

Orcas are called killer whales. Why? Because they eat all kinds of prey—birds, sea turtles, seals, and even sharks.

Orcas can also push a lot of fish into a tight ball. Then the orcas take turns eating the prey. This is called a bait ball.

Super-predators

Biggest

A blue whale is longer than two school buses. But it eats shrimp-like critters no bigger than your pinky!

Fastest on Land

A cheetah can run as fast as a car on the highway. It's faster than any prey.

Fastest in the Air

How does a peregrine falcon catch prey? By diving through the air three times faster than a car on the highway.

Strangest

A fossa looks like a cross between a squirrel and a kitten. It hunts lemurs, birds, crabs, snakes, and more.

Longest Jumper

A cougar has powerful back legs. When it jumps from a high place, this big cat can jump the length of a pickup truck.

Most Beautiful

A sea anemone looks like a flower. But it has tentacles with venom. They can kill fish or shrimp in seconds.

Word Bite

TENTACLE: An arm-like part of an animal used to feel things or catch food

Snakes, Lizards, and Crocodiles

A black timber rattlesnake swallows a mouse.

Snakes kill their prey in different ways. Some snakes have venom in their fangs. The venom paralyzes the animals they catch. Then the snakes swallow the prey whole.

Other snakes don't use venom. The anaconda grabs an animal with its teeth. Then it curls around the prey and squeezes it to death.

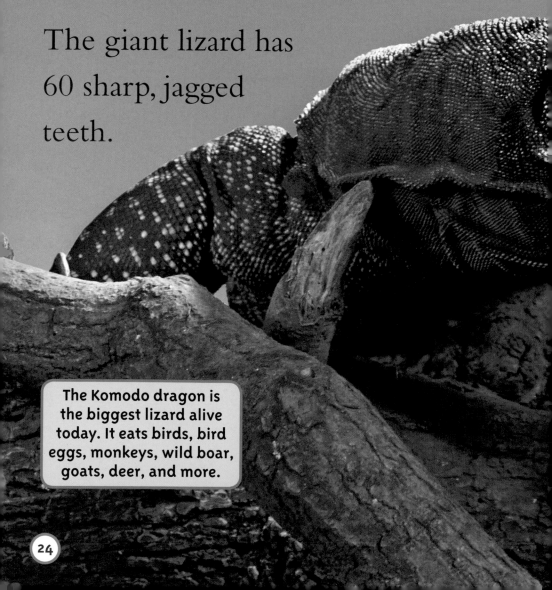

Many lizards are small enough to sit in your hand. But the Komodo dragon is as big as a surfboard.

The giant lizard has 60 sharp, jagged teeth.

The Komodo dragon is the biggest lizard alive today. It eats birds, bird eggs, monkeys, wild boar, goats, deer, and more.

Q What do you get when you cross a kangaroo and a Komodo dragon?

A A leaping lizard.

Its spit is even more deadly. It's full of germs that can kill prey in one bite.

How does a hungry crocodile catch its prey? It lies in the water and waits. The patient hunter can wait for hours.

When prey passes by, the croc grabs it, pulls it underwater, and waits for it to drown.

What does a crocodile eat? Almost anything—fish, birds, snakes, deer, wildebeest (below), and more.

Perfect Predators

Crocs, cheetahs, wolves, sharks, and snakes are some of the most awesome predators on the planet.

But they don't hunt for fun.
They hunt to feed themselves
and their families.

Cheetahs are the fastest animals on land. They eat animals such as gazelles, impalas, hares, and young wildebeest.

Stump Your Parents

Can your parents answer these questions about predators? You might know more than they do!

Answers are at the bottom of page 31.

1

How much meat can some tigers eat at one time?

A. 10 pounds
B. 20 pounds
C. 40 pounds
D. 80 pounds

2

_____ are members of the dog family.

A. Wolves
B. Foxes
C. Coyotes
D. All of the above

3

Which kind of bear is the biggest in the world?

A. Brown bear
B. Black bear
C. Polar bear
D. Sun bear

Which predator sucks out the insides of its prey?

A. A rusty-spotted cat
B. A giant water bug
C. A peregrine falcon
D. A crocodile

Orcas are a kind of _____.

A. Fish
B. Whale
C. Insect
D. Reptile

Which of these animals does not hunt in groups?

A. Polar bear
B. Orca
C. Army ant
D. Lion

Which predator has the most teeth?

A. Gray wolf
B. Giant water bug
C. Great white shark
D. Komodo dragon

PARALYZE: To make unable to move

PREDATOR: An animal that hunts and eats other animals

PREY: An animal that is eaten by another animal

PRIDE: A family group of lions

TENTACLE: An arm-like part of an animal used to feel things or catch food

VENOM: A liquid some animals make that is used to kill or paralyze other animals